# Poems Selected and New

# Poems Selected and New

Heather Spears

Wolsak and Wynn . Toronto

Copyright © Heather Spears, 1998

All rights reserved. No part of this book may be reproduced or transmitted in any form, by any means, electronic or mechanical, without permission in writing from the publisher, except by a reviewer who may quote brief passages in a review. In case of photocopying or other reprographic copying, a licence is required from CANCOPY (Canadian Copyright Licensing Agency), 6 Adelaide Street East, Suite 900, Toronto, Ontario, CANADA M5C 1H6.

Typeset in Palatino, printed in Canada by
The Coach House Printing Company, Toronto

Front cover art: Heather Spears, self portrait, oil, 1962,
       collection Ian Hacking
Cover design: Stan Bevington
Author's Photograph: Dorothy H. Morrison

Some of the new poems have appeared in *The Fiddlehead, Transversions, Kaolonica, Poems for Bosnia (Bloodaxe), The Lancet.*

The publishers acknowledge the support of the Canada Council for the Arts for our publishing program. We also thank the Ontario Arts Council for its support.

Wolsak and Wynn Publishers Ltd.
Don Mills Post Office Box 316
Don Mills, Ontario, Canada, M3C 2S7

Canadian Cataloguing in Publication Data

Spears, Heather, 1934-
  Poems Selected and New
Poems.
ISBN 0-919897-61-4
I. Title.

PS8537.P4P63 1998    C811'.54    C98-932222-X
PR9199.3.S63P63 1998

*for Jay*

CONTENTS

From *Asylum Poems* (1958)
    Now above noise   11
    Now I have lifted   13

From *The Danish Portraits* (1967)
    In the churchyard at Østermarie   17
    The burn scar   18
    The Danish portraits, 3   19
    The Danish portraits, 6   20

From *From the Inside* (1972)
    Elect, predictable, and white ...   23
    Am I so good at it? I tire, ...   24
    (surrealistic, to my head)   25
    What is my sickness? in dreams ...   26

From *Drawings from the Newborn* (1986)
    Hydrocephalus obs.   29
    Asphyxia   30
    Heart-child's father   31

From *How to Read Faces* (1986)
    Fox cubs at play   35
    Viking excavations, Runegaard   36
    The teaching of drawing   37
    Christmas at Christina Lake   38

From *The Word for Sand* (1988)
    Robert Noyes   41
    To my Arabic book   43
    Another refugee poem   44
    From The dolphin in the West Edmonton Mall
        ... The dolphin continues to leap   45
        ... And if I went down on all fours   46
        A separate place for the poor   47
        One night they nearly went
           to the West Edmonton Mall   48

From *Human Acts* (1991)
    Paying attention at poetry readings   53
    Niagara Falls from the air   54
    Night bus to Prince George   55
    How animals see   57
    Bulimia   58
    Refugee swimming, Frederiksberg baths   59
    Human acts   61
    For the soldiers   62
    The poem walked out   63
    News of war   64

From *The Panum Poems* (1996)
    M. temporalis   67
    Biking with skulls through Copenhagen   68

New and uncollected poems
    The woman who drew dead babies   73
    Danny, Oncology   75
    Kasabach-Merritt Syndrome   76
    Jets over Raulands Fjell   78
    Orcas Island, sentimental morning   79
    Poems for Bronwen   83
    The Hay Festival   84
    Mammography Survey, Bispebjerg Hospital   86
    In denial   88
    On cultural expropriation   89
    The light changes   91
    The blind Argentine   92
    Rumania on the BBC   94
    The God poems, 1-9   95
    Modern times   104
    Poem   105
    Quake Poem 1   107
    Quake Poem 2   108
    Drawing at Centennial Pool, Victoria   109
    The search for Scarlett   110

From *Asylum Poems* (1958)

**Now above noise**


Now above noise in the noon-void room,
The night-ward white and until-dusk-tidy
I hide me. Here, closed in by my key
Twice by the stairway shut I bide

On bed to lie me. Below, the welled
Sound makes this still. I loose my shoes, undo
The breastplate apron, pull to me the pillow,
The iron springs interpreting my motion.

Now down I am, bed-bound, by my will
Weighed, held level, lower than I wended,
To ascend the vacant boundaries of the bed,
The bleak ward strange and now oh not friend.

For I am wasted, frailer than I was,
No longer nurse, or nourished by my virtue;
What were sleek wrists now all wrinkles grow
Banded, but I not look, lest I stir.

And head comes haunted, by all forms
Afflicted, I feel their force is urgent,
Denser, the unburning bulb's indifferent
Vague edge now intense is my invader.

And chair has charged significance —
Each leg meeting the large floor is tragic;
Rage to change, shift somehow that thin, thick
Shape assails me, mind aches in its image.

And sharp the taut-drawn sheets, over frames'
Seven-recurring structure fragile fastened
Grieve me; past them window at ward's end
Trembles with bars. Beyond, the massed

Light against the glass presses leaden
And dread goes down me — I turn me lest I listen
To this impending; deaf I turn again
And troubled, find my keys within my fist.

I by a small metal am so cured, secured
By it, the brittle symbol of my wisdom,
That this cool will quells the raving room
And no more mad oh I mock me as I rise.

**Now I have lifted**


Now I have lifted look the lunatic now
Old oh lifted bleating from bed to chair.
See the feeble erect from the sheet brought bare
Body bend like paper at loin and knee.
Now at the nape the seventh cervical see
Holds like knob or nail the frame, see how
Downward the flesh falls, fold on little fold.
Now I have lifted look the lunatic old.

From *The Danish Portraits* (1967)

## In the churchyard at Østermarie

The sky enters the ruined nave,
Flat gravestones, almost as smooth as glass,
Are propped against the walls in the grass.
Outside, a gardener rakes over a new grave.

Somewhere here she has stood in silence,
She would have no one with her, she did not cry,
There was only the priest, reading unhurriedly,
And her face was hardened as if in defence.

There was one incident before it was over:
When he asked her what the baby was,
She said 'I don't know' and he had to pause
And look in his book. Then he told her.

That is an old story now, like the others.
The grass grows, oh yes, the rake whispers.

**The burn scar**


my son Benjamin
drawn on a dark ground
has flesh cold
as green apples is 3 years old
and thin
and round
shouldered like some famine
poster but the eyes
worldly if outsize
in a long semitic face
my brush indicates arms in 4 white lines
then I trace
the unreadable designs
—his 'bad arm' pressed
for coolness maybe against his chest
crimson but icy how it wants to remake
my picture for its own sake
a wound
radiating into sound
skin, radiating into sound
how he screamed then
Ben
jamin

## The Danish portraits, 3

If I cannot do this marvellous thing
My shame will make me cry,
If my hand will not answer me, if my
Eye will not tell me what it is seeing,
I mean you, where you are sitting there
On the high table grayish with old glaze, the
Antique blue wooden clock a crazy
Halo on your incredible hair
Gold ochre straight from the tube
But the shadows God my look is lost
In them, at the most terrible cost
I will wrest their colour out of them, I will do it
Like plunging my hands into blood
But I could not touch you, even if I could

### The Danish portraits, 6

Crouched there, your arms thin gold
Draw in the thin gold limbs under your
Little dress: you are exposed and unsure
And even the colours are cold.
In the day light lying across your hair
Summer has lightened it I can trace
The pallor of your lowered frightened face
A strand of green so cool I can almost hear.

Can it ever hurt you that I shall hide
You here, that I shall in this way
Contain you?  see how my patient hand has
Pushed the encroaching shadow back, and made
Light of your frailty and dismay
On the dark primed passive canvas

From *From the Inside* (1972)

Elect, predictable, and white
the flower of my resolve, I hover just off the earth, the last
nothing. My root is atrophied, it took
too much to produce the bloom, the ice
blossom. I shudder in the wind.
Proud tulips, recall me, your fists of dark
surge, you fling over the sun, gorgeous, your black coagulations.
I have since dwindled. If you would take, eat,
here is the papery leaf, a wafer of petals.

Am I so good at it? I tire,
the fabric gives again, I must mend,
elsewhere and elsewhere the birds soar like stones,
trees live their own lives, and perfectly.

To live my life! that would be something. The appalled
infant stares up at forms of light, its hands
swim vaguely, as against glass, its skull
is warped, hairless, its blue spine
a reed.

Now it is interpreting the shape of the light —
a wound. It is touching, questioning its warm excretions.
Enough. It is folded, smoothed, hushed.
Oh difficult and ingenious, the shuttering of its 2 bald eyes.

(*surrealistic, to my head*)

Like a grove abandoned to the dark
I would contain you,
a town woman
happens to inherit a wood,
she walks slowly around it in the dusk,
then goes away across the landscape.

What is my sickness? in dreams
we are totally surprised.
How could I possibly have constructed
this guessing game? out it leaps,
flings off its clueless wrapping,
a bridal shower planned, planned
somewhere, and I smile till my mouth hurts.

From *Drawings from the newborn* (1986)

♀ Hydrocephalus obs.

I would not have noticed.
All newborn heads
are large, are tender, are strange.
They could be planets, their form
the most difficult abstract in the world.
What is there to see?  She is asleep, her hands
curled at her well-formed face.
And now I trace
and retrace the simple profile of that head
from nape to brow, over and over
as if it were changing, its edge
trembling to change, like water swelling toward light.
Even when I get it right, it will not be right.

**Asphyxia**

So close, the curtained opening
like a low moon occludes her body:
everything is light.
She has not moved. My face
at level with her face, I draw.
Someone turns her, lays her glossy arm
back across her body. Not a finger moves.
In there, inside the glass,
everything is soft, blurred, warm,
only the nasal tube's blue metal
comes sharp, its shapes
beautiful with utility,
that breathes her so perfectly
her chest does not move. Her closed
eyes do not move.
On the screen, the tiny green snake
of her life whips and whips and whips.

**Heart-child's father**

His dark thick wrists
hang from the yellow sleeves, the bibbed
pitiful ties at his shoulders.
He leans forward in the chair, his gaze
fixed on the crib, and the one they call
'the big child'. His face is erased:
the expressive muscles
utterly soft and lax, it is a nothing face
undone, abandoned in its privacy.
The doctor, a woman, bending over the child,
has something to do with her hands.
When at last he stands
to go, he speaks and makes a smile.
He stoops as he passes me, as if he were walking downhill.

From *How to Read Faces* (1986)

## Fox cubs at play

Last night I heard the vixen's
witch-laugh up past the quarry
when I was out with the dog.
The dog's in heat, the cat's
heavy, so wide her whiskers
don't warn her in doorways.
Life's at it.  In the window
the buds on the whitethorn sprig
are slick fat spheres
pushed from the inside, the small cells
busy, very busy.  What's visual now
bores me, that eventual casual green,
but the thought of animal play
repeated a thousandfold, tumbling the country,
in ditches, woods, warrens, and nothing to do with man,
pleases me well.

## Viking excavations, Runegaard

What surprises is
how little there is to see
new nails in rows in the trodden down
clay earth, the squares
and rectangles dug out with their mounds.
A discernible whiteness marks the place
where a head lay, a pelvis:
this has to be pointed out.

Children walk warily
along the graves.
Only one skeleton is intact,
already exposed
up to the femurs, the long bones
decorously straight, striated
and brown as buried wood, the two brown
kneecaps delicately in place, like buttons.

The clay has been coaxed away by tools and fingers;
the archaeologist, standing in the pit,
waters it with a fine spray out of a nozzled can
it darkens
he straightens up, his knees at ground level,
and tells us that Vikings were small, smaller than women.
Away across the field the pinewood hides the shore,
the dig is a meagre space, and windy,
very little has been uncovered.

## The teaching of drawing

a line is
nothing
it is the turning away of a stone, a shoulder
it is the terrified awareness of absence
faltering into consciousness and speaking itself in a whisper
it is this hair, hazardous as grass
it is the ground, your feet splay,
black earth fastens into them.
it is the inside of your mouth
parting on darkness
or your genitals, the perfect detail of accident
it is the abstract of the world
it is the slow recording
of what happens between my eye
and the skin of your neck
averting and tightening
over aeons
it is the gunshot stammer
of flames in bracken
it is the track of an insect
dragging itself painfully by millimetres
across the surface of the cortex
or a yell of pain
finished instantly —
silence of it.
scar of it.

## Christmas at Christina Lake

Falling asleep slowly, the short couch
like an embrace, the quilt soft at my chin,
past my head the one lamp by the table
looks over your shoulder
you are cleaning the oboe, it takes hours,
tiny dismantled parts
spread out on newspaper, your fingers moving among them
no one else awake, no sound
except, sometimes, the small comfortable tick of metal
on metal, as though you were playing a secret game
with intricate rules, and one of them was silence.
And the deep snow
pressing on the roof, pressing on the sills,
and still falling.

From *The Word for Sand* (1988)

**Robert Noyes**

*B.C. Supreme Court, 12-13 February, 1986*

Having drawn you for two days
over and over (the same drawing,
because I sit in the same seat
and because I am accurate)
and now, standing at the bus stop
with the last light
changing the inner contours of the North Shore mountains
the way, at 2 PM, from some high window
it found its way to your cheek and defined
the quivering masseter, muscle of pain,

I realize that I am standing in your body, that my eyes
and hand have taken in more than I intended,
the sullen slope
of your shoulders in the beige corduroy
jacket becomes me, the lifted
narrow chin and the eyes
slightly lowered to compensate —
looking straight ahead —
guarded and candid
blurred and intolerably vulnerable

but it was tolerable: I drew,
the glass wall between you and free people
contained you like an isolette (I am used to this)
there are actually 2 drawings
because sometimes you'd lean forward
and all I saw
was the corduroy pulled across your back
and the crown of your head
and the fingers of one hand
that supported your face.

You have listened to your life
as a series of letters and assessments
by bewildered headmasters
and discomfited psychiatrists
behind which the romping bodies of small boys
the colour of my 'skin-colour' pastel
were allowed to hover
within reach of the memory
that persists in your hands
hanging empty from your wrists

an 'excellent dedicated teacher'
who touched inappropriate people
very inappropriately

angry citizens in badges
are sitting upright behind me
repulsed and fascinated —
in the breaks, their seething for justice
brims into words —

the voice of the lawyer
continues, the judge slumps
and fingers his chin,
you are judged, are here to be judged
'dangerous' —
still in your body my mind speaks:
'By good fortune
I did not hate but
by bad fortune I loved
and fell from grace
like an angel
leaving a red gouge in the sky,
irreparable'

**To my Arabic book**


Dear stupid Teach-Yourself-Arabic book,
I have completed Lesson Five
and you have yet to tell me
the word for arm, or leg, or salt,
but I can write perfectly
*The delegates are at the Ministry.*
I can even write
*The busy, diligent, famous, honest, clean, clever, important*
*thin, fat, lazy*
*delegates are at the Ministry*
and I know the gender agreements and all the duals and plurals
and the words for *war zone,* and *council,* and *factory,* and *government*
but not the word for sand, and wind, and star.

**Another refugee poem**


When he pulls up his sleeve
to show us the scab on his elbow
where he fell off the bicycle
donated by the Refugee Help
and I see again his forearm, striped
with the long combings of luxuriant hair
   I crumple and shout aloud
   I am slung into a sack of dark cloud
   its seams drawn tight with leather thongs
   and diminishing over the rooftops.

My mind blinks, the room is the same
no one has moved, or spoken.
Or, someone said inconsequential words,
perhaps myself.

Is there no other woman
so afflicted? My age
deranges me with sudden lust,
I am powerless, encapsulated.

His sleeve falls back, but his forearm
fumes like lightning's after-image
across my retina. I pour out more tea.
Another year, or two, surely I will have learned
how to be in this marvellous world and not of it.

From **The dolphin in the West Edmonton Mall**

[2]

The dolphin continues to leap
its body is the spout of itself
leaping, its soul
is a muscle, a fountain
poised and falling
the water continues to be disturbed

The people watch and move away
their looks are curious and blank
its leap is without mind
its despair is perfect
its joy is perfect
its cells
spill upward, its fall
repeats itself, around it
the wild birds fall from the ceilings,
perishables, and are replaced (you have told me this)
the water continues to be disturbed

[3]

And if I went down on all fours
(on my knees)
in the West Edmonton Mall
people would accept this also,
and believe I was paid to do it
a performer
because everything is contained here
(you have told me) even obeisances,
there is even a chapel, even
a sunless beach
with nervous, fabricated tides.

[4]  A separate place for the poor

They ought to establish
a special room for the poor
in the West Edmonton Mall
where those
who could not afford
anything
could go in order to fondle things —
furs, for example —
you said
I thought, however,
you were going to say a special room for those who found the
West Edmonton Mall
intolerable
and who could not understand
how they came to be there
and who could wait in this room
until they understood —

There is a chapel, you said.

But a chapel would not suit these fastidious people, or the poor, who would pray for money.

[6]     One night they nearly went to the
        West Edmonton Mall

It was the night the roller coaster
which is called the Mind Bender
broke like a salamander.
Nader Ghermezian
could not be contacted by the press.
Several people in Edmonton
said to each other, Yes,
I went on it yesterday, or, I planned
to go on it tomorrow. And
the newspapers quoted some-
one as saying, Who knows what's going to happen to the Drop of
Doom?

So I never saw that animal
and I did not kneel
in the West Edmonton Mall
I have left that city
perhaps I was too angry
at the dolphin for being happy
and I cannot fathom
what they mean by the Drop of Doom
perhaps it is a tincture
so potent it could fracture
the dolphin's slopping tank
and whatever you ate or drank
would contain its colour
and you could not cure such water,
it tastes of life, it is so bitter.

In the *Edmonton Bullet*
you said, they've always called it
The Killer Mall
So you can call
this the Killer Mall Suite.
And I have never seen
the dolphin.  And I do not think I would have gone.

From *Human Acts* (1991)

## Paying attention at poetry readings

I am always moral
at poetry readings
I pay attention, or I try
I always get lost
I begin to rearrange the hair of the poet
or to trim (or eliminate) his beard
I press his trousers
I am fascinated by his fingers
I love his pleasure and his disarming smile
at a particular phrase
I love the little pieces of paper sticking out of his
books

Some poets are austere
they read impatiently
they frown
they do not ingratiate
they dare you to alter their appearance by one thread
they look at you
suddenly
under this kind of pressure
I am dismayed to find
I have again lost track of what they are saying

It is necessary for the poet
to be present
it is to be hoped
that in an audience of twelve or over
(twelve being a respectable, even apostolic number)
that the poem, having been as it were reborn
foundering among the chairs
will be received here and there
by the large if fallible pale ears of the listeners
cupped for it like hands

### Niagara Falls from the air

says the pilot in a folksy tone
and I find myself
on the wrong side of the plane
(the left-hand passengers craning down,
                              self-satisfied)
dark dead Lake Ontario fills my window as we bank
for the run into Toronto

while Niagara falls from the air ...

in the clear morning, continuously
drop by drop, atom by atom
cascade of landscape
trees with their long shadows
and root systems extended like skirts,
buildings separated into their fragments,
gables and windows
turning in the light, faceted, winking,
fields spilling their snow,
tiny freeways embellishing the distance
like musical signs: diminuendo,
legato ...
and the little people of Niagara falling like tapers
drawing their hair down after them
as candles discipline their flame
in an excess of light

and Niagara falls, falls from the air
behind us, blue, luminous, without termination.
We land. We have landed.
Let us reverently deplane.

## Night bus to Prince George

Two girls got on at Terrace
children, almost, as they passed
I took in,
in this order, their smell
their matted hair, their wretched
packs and clothes.
They sat behind me, talked
like records running down
of a boy one of them 'almost fell for'
and one who 'finished the section for me yesterday'
'Oh him — I wouldn't —'
suddenly both were asleep, upright,
silence from then on.  And the whole time
this smell, recognized instantly,
not cigarettes
or age or illness, just plain sour
animal human dirt —
follicles, cells, pores, the uninhibited skin's
ordinary youth and health.

And as their voices failed in sleep
I thought of the camp — hours on the slope
mosquitos, coughs, a boy calling,
earth under their short nails
grit in the corners of their brilliant eyes
hair shoved back, narrow napes and wrists
scratched from bites and thorns,
then, pissing in the bush,
perfect teeth tearing off bread, squeak and snap
of a Pepsi can,
and the tent, the hard ground
countdown into exhaustion
asleep with their clothes on.

I won't smell this again
perfume of tree planters
it's from away back
it's real
drowsing, I wish
it were not wasted on me, I dream
a young, blind man
in my seat, abandoning
his perfect senses to it all night long
drinking this sweetness in.

**How animals see**

This is terrible.
It says here
bees can't see yellow.
So the broom, the rape, even the dusty
stamen of the rose
are lurid puce, a shuddery ultra pink,
studied to perfection
over hot millennia how best
to please their lust
these bits
zooming in for the take
faceted fuzzy cells
the dancing optics of a vast
seduced intelligence.
And as for us
what the flower intends
is less than casual —
utter indifference.
Oh my notched, loved world, atlas of lies,
no longer fit to believe!
and not even mine, not private —
photographed, reassured —
Van Gogh in Arles —
impassioned cadmiums!
Armfuls of buttercups
plundered in childhood
on the Musqueam flats!
And now this maple, frost of gold!
The bees are gone to hive,
in secret, they keep the real real,
their tiny manifold eye
closing in on
the actual valuable
planet, terrible in neon and violet.

**Bulimia**

is not a nice word
one thinks of
bulbous dimpled arms and bums,
bulk, bulges and bullocks
Bulimia
the medical profession,
men, probably,
could have chosen more courteously
there are lovely words
Islands of Langerhans
where the sky meets the sea
even Leukaemia
lesser goddess, gentle
and Pyorrhoea
although there is something about little fish in it

Bulimia
I'd rather think of Blake
who ate a whole bottle of linseed oil
one evening
simply because it was there
'Work in the morning, eat at night'
he said, and was joyful
nobody told him he was suffering
from Bulimia
he thought he was healthy;
after a matchless life,
he died clapping and singing.

## Refugee swimming, Frederiksberg baths

How easily, dangerously one condescends!
The teacher is a nice, trim Dane,
cropped hair, flat belly, strides
on the tiles, orders us almost apologetically and smiles,
the smallest of signals.
Only we, in the water,
pick it up like seals
with our unerring animal radar.
The big one from Somalia,
her firm black flesh bulging
in the sleeved gym suit, and the pregnant
Iranian with her long hair
streaming on the surface and
(seen in the showers)
the beard
in the small of her back,
combed vertical by the water,
and me, not eligible,
foreign enough to try
and lovely Hind, gasping.

We tread water with a vengeance,
our eyes fixed on our teacher as students ought
but a touch meeker, a touch
(because we have learned) compliant,
responding to that flicker of a sign,
that tiny *Übermensch*
behind her eyes.

Once there was a word
(we are splashing and trying)
— *paternalist* — the Danes
treated 'their' Inuit so —
it's not racism oh no it's not
you need
to be down here in the water to notice it
down here kicking to the count
remembering to breathe
while the walls
gleam and echo to her voice
her niceness, the fact that she'd deny
any of this, and I
too, back in my clothes and
cycling down Gotersgade
my blue eyes
adequate disguise
that glance at dark families shopping on the street
and before I can kill it
change, just
imperceptibly

**Human acts**

Twelve men and boys
taken in a raid
driven to an olive grove away from the village
the orders were to break their arms and legs.
Soldiers who didn't want to do it
could go and sit in the jeep.
As for the last man,
they broke only his arms.
That was / so he could walk back
and tell what happened.

Was it nearly dawn when he got there?
These paths, the twisted road are known to him
like his own hands, like the faces of his children.
He cradles the split arm
with the one he still can move
high against his chest, it has become
outside himself, he could be carrying a lamb
or a child. He whispers.
There is enough light, anyway,
and over this ridge
the village in terrible silence.

**For the soldiers**

Any one of you
could have been my son
your forgivable
glowing skin / I'm proud of
your roving eye
your bear's strength
loose of my old knots
walking out in the world where it's
white and dangerous

I'm off Mom what I do
hasn't to do with you

I'll draw you then
empty as I know how
no regrets, no late advice
(my eye won't tell
what my hand has seen)

slouched by a wall, or on the run
and staring upwards, with all
the obscene paraphernalia —
and what you write
in those abrupt, square
letters building stone by stone
Masada and Jerusalem
I won't read

any more than I can read your eyes
secret and arrogant and no more mine
than Simon, Daniel, Benjamin

## The poem walked out

The poem walked out and it did not
know where to put itself
it entered the eye of a young soldier
and was extinguished.
The boot of a soldier crushed it in the road
several shadows of running children crossed it
it began to speak,
in the noise of gunfire it was interrupted
and changed into little pieces of sound.
A girl lifted it between her fingers
but it withered. The light fell on it
and was blinded. The poem wrote itself
across the back of a man walking
into the hills near Tayasir
no one explained it. All day it clung
between his shoulders, it attempted to comfort him
the poem was not adequate.
It began to be ashamed.
The man took it off and folded it carefully
and put it down.
He sat on a stone beside the poem
with one hand on his knee and one hand
covering the poem. It became dark.

### News of war

The phone, and we're out of sleep
one of the young men
saying irreparable things.
How did I get into this?
You fling yourself against my arms
as if I were a coat
you fling off. Floor, walls, furniture
are as much use. Your face
pulled into its exaggerations, hideous.
Shit, you say in your infallible woman's voice

Shit Denmark, shit Bush, shit the people.
You run from room to room, switching on lights.
I'm trying to get the BBC and you're screaming.

From *The Panum Poems* (1996)

## M. temporalis

If you put your hands to your temples
you will find
them covering up two other hands
forever yours, as much as ever is,

*temporalis*, stretched over the almost windowed mind
as if behind such beaten alabaster
the minnowy temporary tick
of neurons could be counted, visible —

and time
touches first here with its white hair
who knows why? most beautiful
name, and shapely too the way these lie
steep at the caving-in behind the eyes
two simple slips along the bone
and hold the head in secret, and mean no harm.
As if a voice said, *Look, look forward, that
is what is coming,
do not flinch.*

## Biking with skulls through Copenhagen

5: 2 on my back
and 3 on the rack behind me the fingers of my left hand
signing each box through the soft vinyl bag
to steady me, my right hand steering,
upright against all odds and wobbling forward —
not a good plan to run the yellow
today, with such cargo! who'd come
to pick up — wheels spinning
and everything spread, as the other
bikers swerve to avoid bone bits
curved like shells, a scatter of long teeth?
So I'm taking extra care, let the speedy crowd
pass me in brilliance, thread into distances,
my mind's on the near curb, by Panum the patch
of wet cobbles where the bike path
crosses the sidewalk and my gritty hoard
jolts in its gauze, past Sankt Hans Torv
and the concrete ugly fountain
I'd head out casually here,
nip over into Elmegade past the antikvarium
try to make the next light, but instead
I slow, reach back for another ritual touch,
and check the weightless weight across my shoulders.
Past 70s housing and easing round the corner
into Prins Jørgens Gade where once
squatters threw toilets from the fifth floor
windows and then escaped by a tunnel
under the urinals —
all new fronts now, the socialist café,
minor graffiti, fruit stalls, 'habibi'
says the Palestinian to all his customers
the way they say 'love' in London

I won't stop now for his *portughali* here comes
the Number Three behind me, this time
let it pass, wait in its stink at the stop
while the others go streaming by,
more sleek and cautious than I've ever gone,
nearing home and my mind
retells them even now: 2
on my back (infant, child)
3 in a row on the rack
(woman, woman, man)
that makes 5 —
and then I remember
it's 6 actually,
and as valuable.

# New and uncollected poems

### The woman who drew dead babies

The woman who drew dead babies thought of herself in other terms. Had sometimes to go out in the small hours of the night, that time 'when fires break out and children are born.' Was like the illegal midwives in Canada who drove small cars through deserted streets and avoided the hospitals reeking of foreboding and harm. Was like a thief, intent on her own business and no one else's. Was like a detective, or a fireman or anyone who was at the mercy of someone else's timing. Could sometimes be put off but not for long. Was not happy when like an undertaker's help she came too late and had to seem to reconstruct what was already in decay. Was dismayed when even as she drew, the small cheeks, or the skin over the narrow skull, loosened and drooped in folds like wet cloth. Was dismayed to see the large and perfect ones, and wondered (at first curious, no longer) why they had not lived. Was used to standing in cold rooms among shiny equipment. Drew also living babies but was not remembered for that. Had once drawn a baby who died as she drew it, a faint bubble appearing between the lips. Was aware, as those who have watched through a hospital illness are aware, how naked and bereft the prepared dead look without their systems and intubations. Did not prettify, usually, except in the case of torn skin. Had been asked more than once to draw the eyes opened, eyes no mother had ever seen lifted toward her, opening. Endured the tears of parents, was embarrassed, took her money and left. No longer kept letters of gratitude. Had drawn from a black photo while the parents stood at her shoulders and told her what to put down, like a police artist. Had drawn with no photo at all, only their words, their stammered intact memory. Had also drawn a premature head and turned it upright, to resemble a school photo. But the woman who drew dead babies had seldom to accommodate, for the simple reason that parents loved the look of their own child, could love anything.

The woman who drew dead babies had another life that had nothing to do with it. In this life she took holidays, went shopping, felt ordinary. At home, even while drawing, she listened to talk shows on the radio. She often turned the picture (if it was a photograph) upside down or sideways, her own drawing as well. Finished, she stood and stretched, reheated coffee, bustled a little to put the drawing, under tissue paper (blue or pink), into its envelope. When she had cleared up she would go over to the window, open it, notice day or evening, sniff at traffic and grass. The woman who drew dead babies had once dreamed of becoming a real artist.

In the hospitals she was more vulnerable. The idea nowadays was to let the parents sit with the infant while it expired: the tubes were removed; often the baby, comforted by human warmth and no more invasions, clung on for hours. She had drawn babies while the tears of fathers fell across their faces. Heart-babies were always the most beautiful, with black hair and red cheeks. Unusually long eyelashes on the chronically sick — an extravagance, the body's helpless compensation.

The woman who drew dead babies sometimes had to take a while to acknowledge, in her heart, a kind of beauty in the child. Then, in spite of circumstances, she was able to continue.

The woman who drew dead babies was glad that she had never lost a baby herself. Therefore she could not understand and was not forced into trying. She saw that nothing was necessary except to perform the act, which was both compassionate and impartial. She allowed the act to take care of the sentiment 'so there would be no residue.' The woman who drew dead babies had once dreamed of becoming a real artist.

The woman who drew dead babies sometimes laughed, ate chocolate, and read polite mystery novels in bed, careful not to guess at the ending.

## Danny, oncology

It's visible, positive though all the words
say what it's not. *Lacklustre* eyes —
*lightless* with pain. Are you comfortable?
Some question, when he sits
forward from his pillows in a crouch,
and keeps still, less for me
than for, if he moves, the renewed intensity
that watches for him
with an even closer attention.
Drawing, I feel like a trapper hid,
a fisherman — that kind of patience.
He's dressed in a plaid shirt to go home, he's not
biting his lip but that's his stance
every cell held inward every ounce
of his thirteen-year-old wary being
on tenterhooks, whatever those are.
In the hall, a littler child runs shouting past.
Danny speaks then, and with such effort —
'That's my little brother
he's three years old, it's his birthday.
He's always acting up.'
Now there's no breath or inclination
for more. How is it I can know
in his low voice such absolute, unlearned,
wasted love, that I'm made untranquil even now,
remembering?

## Kasabach-Merritt Syndrome

The anticipated twofold name
part Prussian even, the stacked pages and graphs
are beyond me, the blackish photographs,
words like *hemangomia, vascular,*
*primitive angioblast,*
*self-limiting, transient, cosmetic and benign*
and then to scare me: *or*
*morbid and cavernous.*

I turn back to the table the harsh light
where you lie without protest
naked, new born
your skin is gray and ill
like fine sand weightless/ weighed down
your life's violence and possibility
presenting only
in this scattering of dark lesions, visible and terrible.

Described as *warm to the touch,*
*taut, pulsatile, without audible bruit.*
A string of three across your brow
blood-red and shiny, so my pencil
leaps and cringes. More on your belly, your side,
while down your gauzy arm and at your throat
swarm the enlarged and involute:
black, foamy, petrified.

I draw a listless hand
finger by finger, the forgivable
minutiae of nail, knuckle, and on the third, there —
a berry, a sudden ruby!

Ruby. In a word I see you, the air
goes clear as water, you're
bejewelled then, bedecked as with coral
rising, its gems and encrustations
islands of breathing silence, you are star
studded, manifold, and my hand
steadies, my vision
writes indelibly, as with points of diamonds.

*Edmonton, 1998*

## Jets over Raulands Fjell

Three, streaming in over the edge of the *Hardanger*,
      through cloudless air,
one white, one black
the way a bird that lifts the shadow side of its wing
      goes black
one in its sudden veering towards us invisible
against this colourless, brilliant sky.
We stand still, we stare
up from turf reddened in September, from
the decipherable path-trace, the deer track,
to watch them blink from white to black to invisible
at play in their own silence
while their noise, detached from them,
bears in on us like an afterthought
      from the shaken valleys.
There are boys up there, they see this land
tilt and pour over them
like a disc, flattened, its lakes
pressed flat in its blue rock.
They fall upwards, precipitous, they hurl themselves,
perhaps in joy.
Now it is possible to forget where they flew from,
where they might, after these harmless turns, be heading.

## Orcas Island, sentimental morning

1

To walk quietly enough you would have to
die of it/ the mist
closes the points, and closes down
among the trees in long shafts of negative shadow
wherever there is light, there is blindness/ the water
has suspended itself between
breath and planetary breath/ its surface
is less real
than this papery perceptual I extend
to its lost peripheries
even the pleasure craft
Norm's Bayliner darling and the rest
lying at the buoys
almost obliterated
their insect/ lines, black
excrescent motors and killing accessories
wiped of meaning/ atonal/ and past
them somewhere a seal slaps
its tail like a gunshot

No one is walking
on the little wet stones

Clean and good
the ebbing demarcation/ the immense
shoulder of the island forever treed
by some fluke as good as forever

2

Every bullet, says a Knesset dove
that 'finds' Palestinian child pierces my heart
no doubt but the child does not care very much
for the pierced heart
it is not important
nor does he hurt less for that and the tree
falls in such an alien place, in such alien air
it could have been any random
forgivable century, totem or flash storm

You can't make yourself light enough
you cannot, no masked Jain or vegan
not you Daniel
aching for purity as the martyr
aches for meaning and almost always
has to pretend
this is or is not the end/ I can't think
of anyone I'd trust here

To be motionless
is great for a moment and then you get
restless, you can't both stay and
live, it's like being politically correct
a tree does not have to be politically correct

How would you like it if you stood
minding your own
business and somebody sawed you off at the foot
and you fell on your face?
It's all dead wood
anyway says the Parks Leaflet/ all that countable trace

the lodgepole brain
alive only under the bark,
all the way up and the roots
innumerable renewals
winking on and off in the thick soft
nebulæ of humus
and the green with its measured conversions


3

Oh ardent! oh heart!
oh hardhatted
bicyclist in mauve nylon stopping to stare!
the fastidious cedar may not withdraw
from the stare or the saw
or the moist kiss of the woman
eager to propitiate/ who has not learned
there is no propitiation


4

The missile designer from Boeing
saw 2 otters this morning
he's a nice man
his wife walks into town alone
his son
grieves him for no reason
gets good marks but he drinks
and totalled the car
we are far
from war
the yellow ribbon

over at the Legion
is bleached by July's sun


5

Now the mist lifts and I see
smog over Vancouver/ a cruise ship
noses off Saturna and soon
the whale sighting excursion
will silence its horn
the forbidding shudder of its engine
lost behind Pender/ then
its small waves
reach me, lisp and disperse

No more fold in time
for the crone Makaw in the photograph
to meet me from the point with her bent
load of driftwood or the breathless canoe
to emerge and enslave, leaping as it scrapes the shore —
they are no more/ I guess they all
died sad. Oh heart, you can't undo
what you hate to have done.
A red biplane
is almost beautiful
a girl in carefully torn
pants runs in rubber fashionable shoes
with a pink final starfish
drooped on her wrist/ we will read
novels, fish with sounders off Freeman
and at five
gather for Happy Hour

## Poems for Bronwen

abound, and so they ought
we measure
the tick of our own canted play
best against silence / remember
the upturned bike, the stick
thrilling the spokes like a clock
maddened? I cannot join
this justified occasion.

Poems about live poets tend to embarrass them
or their wives.
What did I mean?
It's that habit of invasion
the live don't like, but the dead
can't fend off; they are fair,
deliverable, anybody's version.

At the Lion's Gate (a hospital)
Anne's good left hand wards off
but definitely
proffered books of poetry.
It's gone, she can't attend.
Mild ladies from the United
Church are her cup of tea.
She's angry
at her loss, but what's lost
hurts less unheeded.

Brilliant breathless loving friend,
still all there and to what avail
in your wide, dumbfounded stare
and loud intentional
sigh of relief when I get the chair
outside for one more (one less) sky!

**The Hay Festival, event nr. 159**
*Hay-on-Wye, June 1 1997*

A bird beating about the marquee
while on the platform Erica Jong
adjusts her dark blue
spectacles and Marilyn French
hoists closer her great thick stick
she is lame
it is Jong who voices it
'I wish that bird would be let out'
best line of the day
observant, ecological
while the May gale
slams at the tent and slits of sun
shake and the bird's gestures are lost
in the catcall slap
of guylines and canvas, and under the mats
the red churned earth of the schoolyard
softens

We are hearing about 5 men who control the media
as in 10 Jews who rule the world
and how being refused an article
about doing without makeup
(not to offend the lipstick client)
is worse than BEijing because it is "uinsidious"
and how (incarcerated) Chinese
can't understand the distinction

Crashes!  Will the pegs hold?
Will the whole thing
collapse, catch us in a sacred shambles
of vigorous, elbowing white?

Or will it lift, bellowed,
a bridal canopy, carousel
turning high over the transparent valley,
ropes trailed like frayed lace
and the bird freed and we,
back in the open, gaping, the far wings
fading like faint applause?

## Mammography survey, Bispebjerg Hospital

The signs to get us here
through complex halls and stairs —2 perfect circles side by side
with dots for nipples
and a felt-drawn arrow but ah we are
all otherwise — tired, stretched, flat,
lopsided Bushman-droopy — all day long
our sad fruits two and two
cringe on the tray.
Waiting, we sit in rows
our envelopes held like party invitations,
tea with the awful Queen.
Their crisp brown
may be incendiary
it's our bacon

Mine warms, so neutral and prayer-defeating
look there's a page, a double mandala
clipped to it: 2 circles crossed, 2 pies
labeled L for left and R for right

We try a little chat but mostly
are silent, we are now statistical
not personal: not me, let it not be me
say the statistics but it won't do
will it, or any other magic

We are white-haired
we are slightly more than usually scared.
Pushing our luck to have got this far
who wants to be mugged
getting out of the tram? we have learned
the polite, conciliatory smile.

The one with the husband over there
does not have to look
complacent, he got up with her at seven
how kind, his hearty hand
on her shoulder as she goes
into her cubicle, he'll be there
when she emerges for all to see

We are jealous yet (oh God)
she's no more immune for that —
husbands and comfort can be
erased with a flourish
in front of the Big C

When I leave, the arrows point
behind me, they can also be
turned, written on little paper mandalas
L or R — who'll be back?  Who'll be left
this time next year or next?
is it right after all?
is it all right?

**In denial**

You are in denial, Cordelia, caged bird would you really have
liked his stink in that small space his hoar breath
his interminable scratching at himself
under the filthy garments?
his love?  that's it then, the rest
you could have dealt with, don't we all
dutifully, wishing it otherwise?
Nothing is so satisfactory as a clean young body
nothing repels like an old one
least of all the rude way he was then
weaned off court comforts, moor mucked with,
the heath caught in the rags of his beard and hair
he'd be defecating on the bare stone —
there's odour for you!  glimpse of leathery old shanks
careless, but with love still beckoning
ah could he have stroked you in life as he did
in your death, so pure, and you'd have permitted it
Cordelia, image of the cell, fantastic play within play,
impossible globe of brightness, to contain a whole world!

## On cultural expropriation


As the oppressor desires his victim
she desires
the mind of the aboriginal, it is not
sexual, it is sexual as trees are, softly and attentively
she would occupy
other now than the land — the private territory
the sweat lodge hidden in the bush
what occurs there
the magic and innocence.
She has kept
part of her brain for this, she goes in
ducking her head, the smoke she invents there
soaks her, she believes she is nearing the truth.
She desires
the exact lineaments of that imagined one
stripped and sweating, that one's authentic
darkness
lately she does not enter, she knows
it would not then be authentic
what she wants she cannot have.
She despises those who do field studies
or call them cooperative research, she names
her sources as authors but that is not enough
of course she scorns
workshops in Shamanism she boasts about
the Sami who would not have his poems translated
she is tender to the slightest slight
in conference papers people raced to finish
and did not check for correctness: she knows their heart.
She wants to rebury the bog people.
She wants to be the only guest allowed
in the longhouse, and then to refuse the honour
or not to be allowed
because no guest is allowed.

She wants to obliterate herself
loudly.  She does not want things written about.
She wants to understand, wants access
to a huge body of accurate and sensitive knowledge
she never can utter, she has wished to help
*them* utter it.  But if it is uttered
it is as good as lost, it is no more what it was.
She stands at the contaminated boundary
she has raised, she has done everything she could,
she has even denied her desire.
Still she desires to lie down in the smoke, to rest,
admit it
to feel the brown hands forgiving at her nape,
or curing in the hollows behind her knees.
She does not want to hurt any more, not to hurt
any more.

## The light changes

There's something about a little girl
sitting up in the front seat
of a car in America with her braids neat
maybe with school books in her lap
and looking straight ahead
and her head
hardly clears the window
and she's serious and there's somebody beside her
and it's scary
of course it's legitimate that's her Dad
he picked her up after a dancing lesson
you know it's all right
but she has a vulnerable slightness to her
and the darker figure past her at the wheel
you can't see his face and what if you could
of course it's all right
nine times out of ten (or nine ninety-nine out of a thousand) but
you've heard too much since you got here
there's a kind of watchfulness afloat
admit it, you too read that stuff if you see it printed
and they know this yes it is their gift for you daily
and the interior of the car
gets dark it's a soft hard modern equivalent
of a sorcerer's cave as soon as the light changes
it's going somewhere
what's the matter with your mind?  she'd be yelling
banging at the window she'd just open the door
step out, before the car
begins to slide away, leisurely
everything's all right and you hate
the ones who said maybe it isn't
and yourself for having seen that ordinary child
in an ordinary car in America
and, before you could stop yourself,
done her infinitesimal harm.

## The blind Argentine

Of all the students
the blind Argentine
is perhaps the most politically correct
but you could wish him less
when you see his beautifully blacklashed eyes
two milks, two molluscs
He has joined the diving class
and got his papers
now headed for Race Rocks
with his buddies everyone
young and eager, the false wind
lifting their hair their faces forward in the sun
as the square craft
bumps across the rip
and ahead of them
the lighthouse red and white as a toy
climbs against the Olympics.
Which means nothing to him,
or the diving gear's neon yellow
and red they suit themselves
zipper in he is handed
tank, mask, getting over the aluminium side
of the boat that sparkles in the sun
How brave to go down
into such darkness! for him lacking even
that watery surface glimmer, the soft
ivory of shells underneath, he holds fast
to the hand of his mate, they strike out
into the race, slow and close to turning.

Now they drift over shallows in a trough, a level falling,
anemone, kelp, threads of sea grass
disentangling, combed as between fingers,
they are poured with the contour of the tide, the sluice
deploys them they are brought
unharmed between the juts and boulders.
While against his face the living
element smooths its minerals, innumerable
plankton and phosphorous they impress
the impatient cells of his skin
nothing is lost to him the lurch
of a dull fin far off, a huge side easing over
heard in the nudge and augmentation
of an echo, all sound
thrusts its physical forms against his body,
strokes him, he hears
from out in the strait a mammal clicking and calling.
They move close to chiton, the abalone dirt gray
and stubborn its great foot
clings to the bottom his comrade wrenches it,
bags it and it has no idea of its beauty —
inward argent and azure —
They return with the tide, they are nearing
the concrete wharf of the island,
the current stalls there, its dead pulse reaches him
he is bursting upwards into the sunlit air, the surface —
the dark —

*Lester Pearson College, April 1998*

## Rumania on the BBC

How awful is the awful
happiness of the good,
we have already seen
the unspeakable
orphanage images and now
a cheery British team
repairing drains and painting ceilings
while from their evil cribs
children are filmed being lifted
and hugged, their mouths
stretching into what is necessary —

The speaker with the microphone
is very pretty, and very fast she wants to convey
happiness back to the viewers
some of whom have donated money

Now it is the cribs
hauled into the yard, their peeled
chewed yellow rods and bars
(probably lead, from the look of the kids)
pulled apart in proper fury,
stamped on, heaved piecemeal
up on the pile, their stained
mattresses following and folding
          — they burn like books

Meanwhile back in the wards, rows of
new wooden cribs have replaced them
as if miraculously. Each child
is lifted proudly in. Toys are given.
Their heads stare as the team waves good bye.

**The God poems**

1. Today God is in His Muslim mode

Today God is in His Muslim mode
it is morning He sees
the Dome of the Rock and cannot but be moved
how splendid it looks, He thinks
with the sun gleaming off its fat gold surface
perhaps One ought ...
and the Jews down at the Wall
beating their heads against the hard stone
are not as interesting as they were last night
so scared —
He can't be everywhere at once
As for the Christians
it is very confusing
especially in America
Military Moms are crowding into the churches
and television studios
He will see what He can do about that later
He is tired
What exactly is He tired of, He thinks

2. God at the U.N.

recognizes the Ambassador of Iraq
and several others, the pasty face
of Perez de Cuellar with his long mournful
mouth/ he's the only one
who registers despair
(but he always did,
even as a child, God remembers
and loves him for it)
God recognizes others, after His fashion
the faces of boredom and regret,
congenital suspicion, resigned contempt,
intransigence grown deep into the lines,
plain irritable longing for a cigarette,
and the sliding mask of concern
that sometimes hides, God knows, good men.
God tries once more
to address Himself to the question
which is fairly serious
His speech
was always more or less at fault
even at its best: Issa in Aramaic,
Hosea and Jalaludin,
Miriam under the palm,
Nobody lately. He looks around at
the General Assembly of His attributes
some of whom pray to Him in various ways.
He feels unable to like
so many that he must love
He must pull Himself together, He thinks

3. God at the press conference

'I try to give you information
that's as valid as I can make it'
says a Brigadier-General
and shows on video
an Area Denial Weapon
which is something
even God is not good at
He wishes at times He was

4. God and the target-rich environment

God hearing about the target-rich environment
considers with renewed respect His dumb
creatures, dogs in front of stores whose minds
are stupid and patient, every animal
waiting in abatement, and trees
who translate the wind and even the saw's whine
into their innocence, all silences
and guileless noise the slide
of the encapsulated fish whose cloth
of water fits continuously, the radiant wing
of a blackbird sleeked down as it settles on a wire
its cry
is beautiful to Him He has sealed
their mouths they have no devious wisdom
right now He appreciates them

5. God considers His next incarnation as a tank

Looking at the Kuwaiti border
called by a bewildered soldier
'the toilet of the world'
God begins seriously to consider
His next incarnation
He will become a tank, He thinks,
only tanks
are called *kills* in the briefing
and there are so many of them — He will
ensure His is no different
made in His image
tank incarnate
its kill
will take all other kills upon it
forgive them, it will say of the fortunate
pilot
as it goes up in smoke,
and its elite turret
melts sanguine and incarnadine.

6. God in the eye of the storm

God has gone out of the eye of the shield
and into the eye of the storm He regards
maneuvers (as always
rejecting *Lo here* and *Lo there*)
he would have preferred
old lines but they're blurred
divers fool around after mines
in the churned-up offshore waters
and up against the ruins of Sumer two jets
nestle like chicks
as for the border
it's a mess huge balls of fire
soften the troops God's finger
has no need to write
where funny little tennis balls
arc perfectly and ineffectually
against the gameroom green
and friendly fire
absolves
the nosedown helicopter crew's surprised
embracement to His bosom

7. God and the ultimatum of the rose garden

God looking down on wintry Washington
would not go so far
as to call this the happiest
appellation for use in future textbooks
if any
but He vaguely remembers
doing something similar Himself
in another garden
the consequences of which
are perhaps just coming home to Him

8. God and the bomblets

God's poet-curate Hopkins
praised Him for dappled things
brindled trout and cow but for good reason
(this was some time before)
not coalition shirts, or the camouflage
that was or was not painted on
the roof of Al-Amriah shelter
God airborne sees
His season breathing northwards
over Bahrain
small buds and ecosystems
its habitual advance
impoverished but reasonably stable
He is very broad
minded He turns over in His mind
each trusting seed and sees
that it is good — among
His children there are poets still
He would have liked to incorporate
bomblets too, God knows it was their intent

9. God has fallen into Mutlah Gap

This went unnoticed.
It closes over Him somewhere among
flaring buses, Kuwaiti men
14 - 45 who had been
forced from a mosque.
The traffic is stuck. Airborne, their liberators
are burning them. God cannot
continue. He reaches out in His fall
for one boy, one chary soul.
He has done this time and again,
He is sick of it.
Nameless, They burn.

**Modern times**

Three Bosnian girls smoking in the stair well
outside Life Drawing class
all legs as I go up, and their eyes
bored, not bored — stuck,
turned once too tight like fuses in a fuse box
two years here and they can't speak Danish
Natasha Svetlana Amadra
at a loss for more than words.

We believed we were living in modern times
that this present war was an accident,
not inevitable, that the long
negotiations could affect its outcome we believed
the weapons were not curious but ordinary we saw
as through a glass, red blood fresh on fresh snow,
we believed what occurred was uncertain, qualified,
that the brother who climbed the hill
could have lived, it took years
before we realized our mistake
before we could see
this day, this worn white stair,
this half-dark February, rain on the skylight, smoke
spiralling upward from the cigarettes
the eyes, the stammered words
were no more capable of other endings
than the wire embedded in the uniform in a brown
1914 textbook photo, or the flint,
or the spear at the museum.

*Svendborg, February 1995*

# Poem

*Missing*: Dorothy Livesay's mail has been returned to the LCP office
with address unknown. If anyone knows where she is, please let us know.
—*LCP Newsletter, July 1996*

This is about the saddest thing I have ever heard,
today anyway and having myself become
somehow as in one leap an Older Poet
I feel it worse, for she was famous.
Is. Famous. The Home on Fairfield, obviously,
refusing all the useless newsletters and muse
letters, returning the muse, They are not a —
well Dee, you had your innings, time shows
on us all, take the AGM it's most painful
with the strident young ones, who as yet
don't know it will happen, and then the next year
you see them and it's happened, something
gone off, hair loss and a bewildered look, as if
they half know it and don't know it.
I don't know it. Listen, I'm 63 and I'm still surprised.
Dee turned beautiful, which is some compensation.
The iron bosom shrank, the belligerent chin
(made more terrible by the tiny mouth, fissure in granite)
dwindled, refined itself, the grating voice dropped to a whisper.
On Galiano, walking through blackberry paths
when I'd complained about an affair gone sour,
she turned like an oracle:
'Heather, it is Time for You to Love a Woman.'
Having earned the right to pronounce. Ah, those secretaries,
their ideals then, their tears,
and the little house on Active Pass awash and hopeless with
 papers, muse
letters arriving, being lost, being filed, memoirs,
remembrances. Her son on the beach, an anthropologist,
 picking up
worked jade among the pebbles, saying it came from Japan,
his own child skipping stones, indifferent.

Where are you?  Last time I saw you I traced
your profile as you slept; the drawing looks
like a mask, but beautiful, you drifted,
wanted — when you opened your eyes — to be taken home.
'There is a lady you would like to meet, an artist —
she lives   I believe in Denmark — ' spoken with great effort.
Where then?  on the edge, the shore,
away out west there with a clean wind for a clean passage, here
I am using the old poetic metaphors
that have been used over and over, Dee,
done to
death

## Quake poem 1

It was the year, or the day, previous.
Premonitions counted for nothing,
those who were afraid
had other reasons: estrangements,
broken promises, they contemplated
moving to Meadowlark Saskatchewan, said to be
the planet's most stable habitation
they did nothing though they read
the literature in the phone book and resolved
to store distilled water, enough for 72 hours
and so on. Others continued to walk around calmly
on the surface,
children, called 'juveniles',
played thoughtlessly under bridges.
Those lying in meadows had the best
chances, a shudder of grasses
poppy flower and pollen loosened across them
and then the grimace
on the face of things
the tectonic wince deeper than foundations
swallowing wells and systems inward, an inversion
a stuck interval
ringing its harmonies
while at the edge of the field
the trees heave, as if about to be sick.

### Quake poem 2

The season I spent in Victoria
which was or was not the last one before the earthquake
was not a good one for the dogwood
only a few patchy flat blooms
but the arbutus
which was suffering some kind of blight
took heart and curdled with flowers
and of course the broom
having mastered the garry oak meadows
the clear cuts and slashed banks
flared its garish curbside yellow
and a tourist from Australia
called it the rabbit of Vancouver Island.

I was sorry to leave in August
just as the plane lifted
getting (as they say) safely airborne
the strip underneath suddenly folded
like a book between the kneeling forests —
or might as well have.

# Drawing at Centennial Pool, Victoria

Ogle or goggle
the poor prof by the pool
at Toronto U of T
would not have been prosecuted if found
busy with a pencil
I know

He had thick glasses
he need not get in
his short eyed, singular audacity
swam through molecular soup
wherever he was
in the grips of Brownian movement his own
floaters covered his corneas whatever
he hoped to see

Round bums and bosoms — why not?
why are the women angry? is Leonardo's
theory of sight as an act, an attack of particles
to be resurrected? Surely it is
only to receive, receive, I am rescued
by innocent paper, my hand
absorbed in its inward workings, my mind
elsewhere than on them — or so they think.

## The search for Scarlett

Not one yet
among all these so sharp with want
so many so many and wrong
yet she exists, somewhere,
she is Tess among the sheaves she is
rising in Africa her eyes bolts
out of the blue the dune hides her
she is in the street in Stockholm
she turns on her blond heel at the next corner
she is in school pouting with boredom
her mouth forms over the pencil
a lovely O
O she is there all right she is
superb, undeniable, when she walks
into the studio they will all shut up
aghast all these gaunt girls
everyone will know her
she will not walk into the studio
she is in Russia
she has a rough cape over her shoulder
she is hidden in Dublin, she is not old enough
wait two years and she will burn
with her two red cheeks and two round breasts
she is learning in a back road in Cambodia her family
will send her into the city she will send them money
they know her worth she is in a library
in Boston and has not yet considered
this seriously she is serious she wipes her glasses and looks
blurredly past her thick lashes
her hair is Gaelic she is getting out of the Shetlands
it clouds her she twists it back she struts
to the bus-stop her clothes are all wrong
but all right anyway it's the way
of her it's Central America

she is going to die before she makes it
it's Sarajevo
Sarajevo says my printer over and over
printing out poems its lights squeeze open and shut
the lights have another purpose she is mute
she is Muslim the child she will bear
is a Serb if it lives
she flings her look she is in a cave
she is under a bridge she is afraid
of an aeroplane
she is laughing the big moon
smooths her big limbs she has lost Tara
Tara of the plains Tara of the sandbank
Tara of the terrible southern marshes
Tara of the city
she has no substitute
she will be difficult to locate
she is probably black
she is not a pretender
you have to go to her
she will not come, search on she is some
where